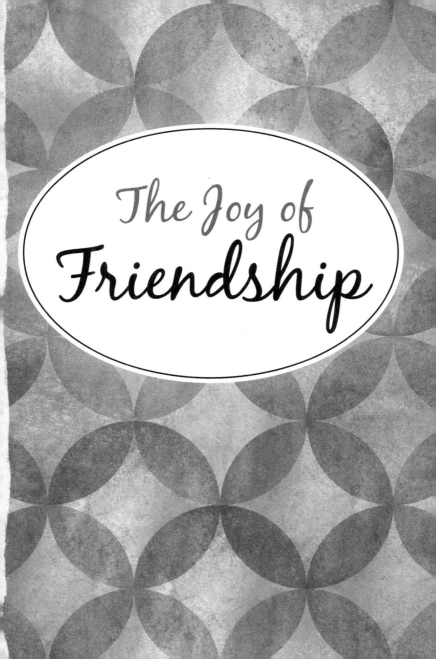

The Joy of
Friendship

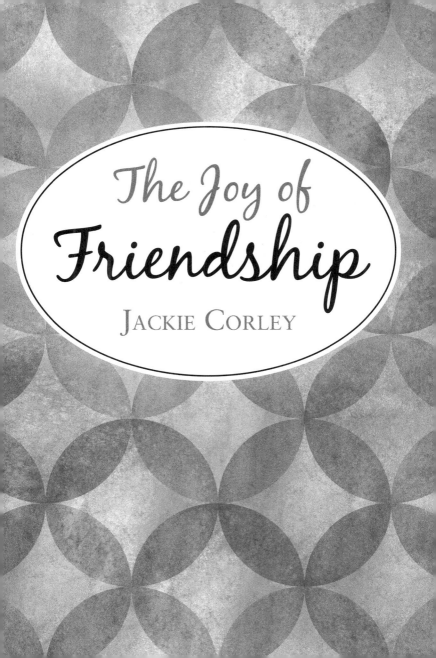

The Joy of Friendship

JACKIE CORLEY

The Joy of Friendship

Text Copyright © 2018 Hatherleigh Press

Library of Congress Cataloging-in-Publication Data
is available.
ISBN: 978-1-57826-760-6

DESIGN BY CAROLYN KASPER

Contents

Introduction

A FRIENDSHIP IS ONE of life's great pleasures. A friend laughs with us, confides
in us, and supports us, no matter the
circumstance.

What marks a friendship? Perhaps
it's the unique connection not bound by
obligation or family ties. That's not to
say we don't feel an obligation toward
our friends or that a sibling or relative
can't be a friend. Simply, friendship is a
relationship we choose and one we sustain with a charitable spirit, patience, and
understanding.

This book collects quotes from poets, scientists, philosophers, and artists as they reflect on the value and character of friendship. The selections explore the acceptance and understanding we find from a friend and why true friendship is often rare. Other quotes dive into some of the hallmarks of friendship: unadorned honesty and fierce loyalty. Still other selections mine the priceless treasure we call a true friend.

A Unique Connection

Friendship is a rare, unique connection between two people, transcending time and distance. A friend meets us where we are in life.

A real friendship should not fade as time passes, and should not weaken because of space separation.

—John Newton

*F*riendship, compounded of esteem and love, derives from one its tenderness and its permanence from the other.

—Samuel Johnson

*N*o love, no friendship, can cross the path of our destiny without leaving some mark on it forever.

—Francois Mauriac

*W*e are like islands in the sea, separate on the surface but connected in the deep.

—William James

*T*rue happiness consists not in the multitude of friends, but in the worth and choice.

—*Ben Jonson*

*T*he pieces I am, she gather them and gave them back to me in all the right order.

—*Toni Morrison*

*R*eal friendship or love is not manufactured or achieved by an act of will or intention. Friendship is always an act of recognition.

—*John O'Donohue*

A friend knows the song in my heart and sings it to me when my memory fails.

—*Donna Roberts*

*A*gain and again, I learn how much friendship enriches my life, bringing warmth, assurance, humour, inspiration, a sense of security. It depends on honesty, trust, loyalty. It's about giving. It's for sharing the good times, but also the tough times, hurt, grief, sadness.

—*Quentin Bryce*

*A*nybody can look at you. It's quite rare to find someone who sees the same world you see.

—John Green

*F*riendship needs no words—it is solitude delivered from the anguish of loneliness.

—Dag Hammarskjold

*B*e courteous to all, but intimate with few.

—George Washington

*T*here is one friend in the life of each of us who seems not a separate person, however dear and beloved, but an expansion, an interpretation, of one's self, the very meaning of one's soul.

—*Edith Wharton*

*W*hen you learn to live for others, they will live for you.

—*Paramahansa Yogananda*

*Y*ou can't choose between Love and Friendship. They're like a package: You either get both or you lose both.

—*Jaejoong*

Age appears best in four things: old wood to burn, old wine to drink, old friends to trust and old authors to read.

—*Francis Bacon*

God, how we get our fingers in each other's clay. That's friendship, each playing the potter to see what shapes we can make of each other.

—*Ray Bradbury*

Friendship however is a plant which cannot be forced -- true friendship is no gourd spring up in a night and withering in a day.

—*Charlotte Bronte*

The only true currency in this bankrupt world are the moments you share with someone when you're uncool.

—Cameron Crowe

Everyone calls himself a friend, but only a fool relies on it: nothing is commoner than the name, nothing rarer than the thing.

—Jean de La Fontaine

Friendship that possesses the whole soul, and there rules and sways with an absolute sovereignty, can admit of no rival.

—Michel De Montaigne

*B*e slow in choosing a friend, slower in changing.

—Benjamin Franklin

*A*re not lifelong friendships born at the moment when at last you meet another human being who has some inkling (but faint and uncertain even in the best) of that something which you were born desiring, and which, beneath the flux of other desires and in all the momentary silences between the louder passions, night and day, year by year, from childhood to old age, you are looking for, watching for, listening for?

—C.S. Lewis

"We'll be Friends Forever, won't we, Pooh?' asked Piglet.
'Even longer,' Pooh answered."

—A.A. Milne (Winnie-the-Pooh)

Friendship needs both confidences and confidence in the other's outstretched hand.

—Anne Roiphe

When twilight drops her curtain down And pins it with a star Remember that you have a friend Though she may wander far.

—L.M. Montgomery

Nobody sees a flower—really—it is so small it takes time—we haven't time—and to see takes time, like to have a friend takes time.

—Georgia O'Keeffe

What if all everybody needed in the world was to be sure of one friend?

—Richard Russo

The companions of our childhood always possess a certain power over our minds which hardly any later friend can obtain.

—Mary Wollstonecraft Shelley

Honesty

FRIENDS DON'T TELL US what we want to hear. They tell us what we need to know. One of the most endearing qualities of a close friendship is honest feedback told with compassion and love.

The key to intimacy is the commitment to honesty and to the radical forgiveness necessary in order for honesty to be safe.

—Marianne Williamson

*T*o throw away an honest friend is, as it were, to throw your life away.

—*Sophocles*

*C*herish the friend who tells you a harsh truth, wanting ten times more to tell you a loving lie.

—*Robert Breault*

*F*riendship that insists upon agreement on all matters is not worth the name. Friendship to be real must ever sustain the weight of honest differences, however sharp they be.

—*Mahatma Gandhi*

*T*he greatest trust between man and man is the trust of giving counsel.

—*Francis Bacon*

*I*gnorance is always ready to admire itself. Procure yourself critical friends.

—*Nicolas Boileau-Despreaux*

*S*ometimes, all it takes is a little honesty between friends. If we gently and lovingly explain what we need from the relationship during our time of grief, and what we are willing to do in return, we can turn even a lukewarm friendship into something special.

—*Margaret Brownley*

There are three friendships which are advantageous, and three which are injurious. Friendship with the upright; friendship with the sincere; and friendship with the man of much observation: these are advantageous. Friendship with the man of specious airs; friendship with the insinuatingly soft; and friendship with the glib-tongued: these are injurious.

—*Confucius*

An acquaintance merely enjoys your company, a fair-weather companion flatters when all is well, a true friend has your best interests at heart and the pluck to tell you what you need to hear.

—*E.A. Bucchianeri*

*T*he best mirror is an old friend.

—*George Herbert*

I love a friendship that flatters itself in the sharpness and vigor of its communications.

—*Michel De Montaigne*

*D*o you know what the difference is between Friendship and Love? Friendship is the photograph, Love is the oil painting.

—*Frank Delaney*

Whoever is careless with the truth in small matters cannot be trusted with important matters.

—Albert Einstein

A friend is a person with whom I may be sincere. Before him I may think aloud.

—Ralph Waldo Emerson

Tis a great confidence in a friend to tell him your faults; greater to tell him his.

—Benjamin Franklin

*H*onesty and openness is always the foundation of insightful dialogue.

—*bell hooks*

*S*eek not the favor of the multitude; it is seldom got by honest and lawful means. But seek the testimony of few; and number not voices, but weigh them.

—*Immanuel Kant*

*O*h, the comfort—the inexpressible comfort of feeling safe with a person—having neither to weigh thoughts nor to measure words, but pouring them all right out, just as they are, chaff and grain together.

—*Dinah Maria Murlock Craik*

We always see our worst selves. Our most vulnerable selves. We need someone else to get close enough to tell us we're wrong. Someone we trust.

—David Levithan

I'd rather have friends who care than friends who agree with me.

—Arlo Guthrie

People love honesty. Honesty is medicinal, I think. It makes people feel less lonely in the world.

—Brad Listi

*F*riendship is the hardest thing in the world to explain. It's not something you learn in school. But if you haven't learned the meaning of friendship, you really haven't learned anything.

—*Muhammad Ali*

*H*onesty and vulnerability endear us to people; they don't endanger us in our relationship.

—*Max Lucado*

*M*y number one commitment to my close friends is to offer the truth as best as I can perceive it and as best as I can convey it. I owe this at the cost of the friendship, itself, because a friend is more important than a friendship.

—Alan Robert Neal

*T*rust and honesty is an investment you put in people.

—Rachel Scott

*F*riends are supposed to act like harbor boats—let you know if you're off course.

—Rebecca Wells

A doubtful friend is worse than a certain enemy. Let a man be one thing or the other, and we then know how to meet him.

—*Aesop*

R eal friends require honesty, openness, and even vulnerability. They also require attention and simple acts of kindness.

—*Mary Pipher*

I f honesty is the key to intimacy, it means we don't have to be perfect and we don't have to pretend to be perfect.

—*Donald Miller*

The Gift of
Friendship

FRIENDSHIP ENRICHES OUR LIVES, infusing joy and laughter in times of sadness and trouble. To have a true friend is to be given a gift.

C lose friends are truly life's treasures. Sometimes they know us better than we know ourselves. With gentle honesty, they are there to guide and support us, to share our laughter and our tears. Their presence reminds us that we are never really alone.

—Vincent Van Gogh

*T*he greatest sweetener of human life is friendship.

—*Joseph Addison*

*T*he tender friendships one gives up, on parting, leave their bite on the heart, but also a curious feeling of a treasure somewhere buried.

—*Antoine de Saint-Exupery*

*I*t is not, as somebody once wrote, the smell of corn bread that calls us back from death; it is the lights and signs of love and friendship.

—*John Cheever*

"Stay" is a charming word in a friend's vocabulary.

—Louisa May Alcott

In the sweetness of friendship let there be laughter, and sharing of pleasures. For in the dew of little things the heart finds its morning and is refreshed.

—Khalil Gibran

Friendship makes prosperity more brilliant, and lightens adversity by dividing and sharing it.

—Marcus Tullius Cicero

*E*veryone has a gift for something, even if it is the gift of being a good friend.

—*Marian Anderson*

*T*he better part of one's life consists of his friendships.

—*Abraham Lincoln*

*W*e are each the star of our own situation comedy, and, with luck, the screwball friend in somebody else's.

—*Robert Breault*

*T*here is nothing on this earth more to be prized than true friendship.

—Thomas Aquinas

A single rose can be my garden; a single friend, my world.

—Leo F. Buscaglia

*S*ome friends leave footprints in your heart.

—Eleanor Roosevelt

*F*lowers are lovely; love is flower-like; Friendship is a sheltering tree; Oh the joys that came down shower-like, Of friendship, love, and liberty, Ere I was old!

—Samuel Taylor Coleridge

I find friendship to be like wine, raw when new, ripened with age, the true old man's milk and restorative cordial.

—Thomas Jefferson

*W*e cannot tell the precise moment when friendship is formed. As in filling a vessel drop by drop, there is at last a drop which makes it run over; so in a series of kindnesses there is at last one which makes the heart run over.

—*Ray Bradbury*

*W*hat are the odds so long as the fire of the soul is kindled at the taper of conviviality, and the wing of friendship never molts a feather?

—*Charles Dickens*

*T*he capacity for friendship is God's way of apologizing for our families.

—*Jay McInerney*

*C*lose friendships are one of life's mira-cles-that a few people get to know you deeply, all your messy or shadowy stuff along with the beauty and sweetness, and they still love you. Not only still love you, but love you more and more deeply.

—*Anne Lamott*

*T*he greatest gift of life is friendship, and I have received it.

—*Hubert H. Humphrey*

*G*old is the gift of vanity and common pride, but flowers are the gift of love and friendship.

—Franz Grillparzer

*N*o soul is desolate as long as there is a human being for whom it can feel trust and reverence.

—George Eliot

*O*f all the gifts that wise Providence grants us to make life full and happy, friendship is the most beautiful.

—Epicurus

And we find at the end of a perfect day,
the soul of a friend we've made.

—*Carrie Jacobs-Bond*

Inner values like friendship, trust, honesty
and compassion are much more reliable
than money—they always bring happiness
and strength.

—*Dalai Lama*

Many kinds of fruit grow upon the tree
of life, but none so sweet as friendship;
as with the orange tree its blossoms and fruit
appear at the same time, full of refreshment
for sense and for soul.

—*Lucy Larcom*

Ah, how good it feels! The hand of an old friend.

—*Henry Wadsworth Longfellow*

Each friend represents a world in us, a world possibly not born until they arrive, and it is only by this meeting that a new world is born.

—*Anaïs Nin*

Hold a true friend with both your hands.
—*Friedrich Nietzsche*

*F*riends make life a lot more fun.
—*Charles R Swindoll*

*W*e need old friends to help us grow old and new friends to help us stay young.
—*Letty Cottin Pogrebin*

*H*ow rare and wonderful is that flash of a moment when we realize we have discovered a friend.

—*William Rotsler*

*I*n all holiest and most unselfish love, friendship is the purest element of the affection. No love in any relation of life can be at its best if the element of friendship be lacking. And no love can transcend, in its possibilities of noble and ennobling exaltation, a love that is pure friendship.

—*Henry Clay Trumbull*

I am quite sure that no friendship yields its true pleasure and nobility of nature without frequent communication, sympathy and service.

—*George Edward Woodberry*

*T*rue friendship is like sound health; the value of it is seldom known until it be lost.

—Charles Caleb Colton

*T*o what gods is sacrificed that rarest and sweetest thing upon earth, friendship? To vanity and to interest.

—Guillaume-Chretien de Lamoignon
de Malesherbes

*F*riendship is something in the soul. It is a thing one feels. It is not a return for something.

—Graham Greene

The making of friends, who are real friends, is the best token we have of a man's success in life.

—Edward Everett Hale

I think in all of us there is a profound longing for friendship, a deep yearning for the satisfaction and security that close and lasting friendships can give.

—Marlin K. Jensen

Friendship inspires and enriches the lives of those who come together.

—Vimala Thakar

Some people need a red carpet rolled out in front of them in order to walk forward into friendship. They can't see the tiny outstretched hands all around them, everywhere, like leaves on trees.

—*Miranda July*

The greatness of a man is not in how much wealth he acquires, but in his integrity and his ability to affect those around him positively.

—*Bob Marley*

Without friends, no one would want to live, even if he had all other goods.

—*Aristotle*

The best things in life are free. And it is important never to lose sight of that. So look around you. Wherever you see friendship, loyalty, laughter, and love...there is your treasure.

—Neale Donald Walsch

Few delights can equal the presence of one whom we trust utterly.

—George MacDonald

*B*lessed are they who have the gift of making friends, for it is one of God's best gifts. It involves many things, but above all, the power of going out of one's self, and appreciating whatever is noble and loving in another.

—*Thomas Hughes*

*I*f you're trusted and people will allow you to share their inner garden...what better gift?

—*Fred Rogers*

Loyalty

FRIENDS WILL HAVE OUR backs no matter the challenges we face. A friendship is defined by loyalty.

The proper office of a friend is to side with you when you are in the wrong. Nearly anybody will side with you when you are in the right.

—Mark Twain

I value the friend who for me finds time on his calendar, but I cherish the friend who for me does not consult his calendar.

—Robert Breault

L oyalty is what we seek in friendship.
—Marcus Tullius Cicero

T he necessity of loyalty between friends, the responsibility that the strong owe the infirm, the illusion of ill-gotten gain, the rewards of hard work, honesty, and trust-these are enduring truths glimpsed and judged first through the imagination, first through art.

—Michael Dorris

*I*f loyalty is, and always has been, perceived as obsolete, why do we continue to praise it? Because loyalty is essential to the most basic things that make life livable. Without loyalty there can be no love. Without loyalty there can be no family. Without loyalty there can be no friendship. Without loyalty there can be no commitment to community or country. And without those things, there can be no society.

—Eric Felten

*R*eprove your friend privately, commend him publicly.

—Solon

*I*f I had to choose between betraying my country and betraying my friend, I hope I should have the guts to betray my country.

—E. M. Forster

I shall remain your friend even if you act contrary to my convictions, and I shall help you even if I disagree with you.

—Milan Kundera

*F*riendship close its eye, rather than see the moon eclipst; while malice denies that it is ever at the full.

—A. W. Hare

A true friend is someone who is there for you when he'd rather be anywhere else.

—*Len Wein*

T rust is the core of human relationships, of gregariousness among men. Friendship, a puzzle to the syllogistic and critical mentality, is not based on experiments or tests of another person's qualities but on trust. It is not critical knowledge but a risk of the heart which initiates affection and preserves loyalty in our fellow men.

—*Abraham Joshua Heschel*

Support your friends—even in their mistakes. But be clear, however, that it is the friend and not the mistake you are supporting.

—Hugh Prather

Success rests not only on ability, but upon commitment, loyalty, and pride.

—Vince Lombardi

You will find joy, frustration and sorrow in your quest. Never forget that friendship and loyalty are more precious than riches.

—Brian Jacques

I think if I've learned anything about friendship, it's to hang in, stay connected, fight for them, and let them fight for you. Don't walk away, don't be distracted, don't be too busy or tired, don't take them for granted. Friends are part of the glue that holds life and faith together. Powerful stuff.

—*Jon Katz*

A real friend is one who walks in when the rest of the world walks out.

—*Walter Winchell*

*L*ove is friendship that has caught fire. It is quiet understanding, mutual confidence, sharing and forgiving. It is loyalty through good and bad times. It settles for less than perfection and makes allowances for human weaknesses.

—*Ann Landers*

*T*he best things in life are never rationed. Friendship, loyalty, love do not require coupons.

—*George Hewitt Myers*

A true friend freely, advises justly, assists readily, adventures boldly, takes all patiently, defends courageously, and continues a friend unchangeably.

—William Penn

A friend's loyalty lasts longer than their memory. Over the course of a long friendship, you might fight with your friend, even get angry with them. But a true friend will forget that anger after a while, because their loyalty to their friend outweighs the memory of the disagreement.

—Matthew Reilly

*W*hat's most important in a friendship?
Tolerance and loyalty.

—*J K Rowling*

*L*oyalty is the pledge of truth to oneself
and others.

—*Ada Velez*

*L*ack of loyalty is one of the major causes
of failure in every walk of life.

—*Napoleon Hill*

A friend is one with whom you are comfortable, to whom you are loyal, through whom you are blessed, and for whom you are grateful.

—*William Arthur Ward*

C ourage and kindness, loyalty, truth, and helpfulness are always the same and always needed.

—*Laura Ingalls Wilder*

W here true fortitude dwells, loyalty, bounty, friendship and fidelity may be found.

—*John Gay*

One loyal friend is worth ten thousand relatives.

—Euripides

It's the friends you can call up at 4 a.m. that matter.

—Marlene Dietrich

Support

FRIENDS GIVE US STRENGTH in times of trouble. They walk beside us, lifting us up when life knocks us to our knees.

The best time to make friends is before you need them.

—Ethel Barrymore

*F*riends share our pain and touch our wounds with a gentle and tender hand.

—*Henri Nouwen*

*T*he bird a nest, the spider a web, man friendship.

—*William Blake*

*H*e that is thy friend indeed,
    He will help thee in thy need:
If thou sorrow, he will weep;
If thou wake, he cannot sleep:
Thus of every grief in heart
He with thee doth bear a part.
These are certain signs to know
Faithful friend from flattering foe.

—*William Shakespeare*

Sometimes being a friend means mastering the art of timing. There is a time for silence. A time to let go and allow people to hurl themselves into their own destiny. And a time to prepare to pick up the pieces when it's all over.

—Octavia Butler

In prosperity our friends know us; in adversity we know our friends.

—John Churton Collins

Friendship is like those ancient altars where the unhappy, and even the guilty, found a sure asylum.

—Sophie Swetchine

*F*riendship that flows from the heart cannot be frozen by adversity, as the water that flows from the spring cannot congeal in winter.

—*James F Cooper*

*W*eddings and funerals are when you figure out who your real friends are.

—*Amy Dickinson*

*T*wo are better than one, because they have a good reward for their labor. For if they fall, the one will lif' up his fellow, but woe to him that is alone when he falleth, for he hath not another to help him up.

—*John Steinbeck*

N o man can be happy without a friend, nor be sure of his friend till he is unhappy.

—*Thomas Fuller*

A good friend is a connection to life—a tie to the past, a road to the future, the key to sanity in a totally insane world.

—*Lois Wyse*

F riendship multiplies the good of life and divides the evil.

—*Baltasar Gracian*

*T*he most I can do for my friend is simply
be his friend.

—*Henry David Thoreau*

*T*he only true test of friendship is the time
your friend spends on you.

—*John Marsden*

*D*on't flatter yourself that friendship authorizes you to say disagreeable things to your intimates. The nearer you come into relation with a person, the more necessary do tact and courtesy become. Except in cases of necessity, which are rare, leave your friend to learn unpleasant things from his enemies; they are ready enough to tell them.

—*Oliver Wendell Holmes Sr.*

*A*nything that's human is mentionable, and anything that is mentionable can be more manageable. When we can talk about our feelings, they become less overwhelming, less upsetting, and less scary. The people we trust with that important talk can help us know that we are not alone.

—*Fred Rogers*

Walking with a friend in the dark is better than walking alone in the light.

—*Helen Keller*

You know a real friend? Someone you know will look after your cat after you are gone.

—*William S. Burroughs*

The friend who holds your hand and says the wrong thing is made of dearer stuff than the one who stays away.

—*Barbara Kingsolver*

A friend is someone who knows where all your bodies are buried. Because they're the ones who helped you put them there. And sometimes, if you're really lucky, they help you dig them back up.

—*Jenny Lawson*

I 'll lean on you and you lean on me and we'll be okay.

—*Dave Matthews*

F riends show their love in times of trouble, not in happiness.

—*Euripides*

*T*he friend who cares makes it clear that whatever happens in the external world, being present to each other is what really matters. In fact, it matters more than pain, illness, or even death.

—*Henri Nouwen*

*O*ur triumphs seem hollow unless we have friends to share them, and our failures are made bearable by their understanding.

—*James Rachels*

*T*hus nature has no love for solitude, and always leans, as it were, on some support; and the sweetest support is found in the most intimate friendship.

—*Marcus Tullius Cicero*

*T*rue friendship is like the asphalt of life. It fills in the potholes and makes the journey smooth.

—*Richard G. Scott*

True friends see who we really are, hear our words and the feelings behind them, hold us in the safe harbor of their embrace, and accept us as we are. Good friends mirror our best back to us, forgive us our worst, and believe we will evolve into wise, wacky, and wonderful old people. Dear friends give us their undivided attention, encourage us to laugh, and entice us into silliness. And we do the same for them. A true friend gives us the courage to be ourselves because he or she is with us always and in all ways. In the safety of such friendships, our hearts can fully open.

—Sue Thoele

*F*riendship is like love at its best; not blind but sympathetically all-seeing; a support which does not wait for understanding; an act of faith which does not need, but always has, reason.

—*Louis Untermeyer*

*B*ut if the while I think on thee, dear friend,
All losses are restored and sorrows end.

—*William Shakespeare*

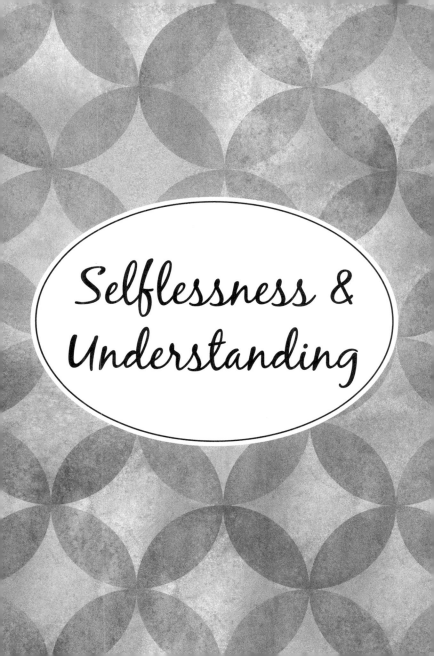

Selflessness & Understanding

FRIENDS ACCEPT US FOR who we are and understand the nature of our character. This understanding is often heralded by selfless acts and generosity of spirit.

*F*riends are those rare people who ask how we are, and then wait to hear the answer.

—*Ed Cunningham*

*O*ne of the most beautiful qualities of true friendship is to understand and to be understood.

—*Lucius Annaeus Seneca*

*F*riendship must never be buried under the weight of misunderstanding.

—*Sri Chinmoy*

*T*here's something beautiful about finding one's innermost thoughts in another.

—*Olive Schreiner*

*O*ur most difficult task as a friend is to offer understanding when we don't understand.

—*Robert Breault*

*D*on't walk behind me; I may not lead. Don't walk in front of me; I may not follow. Just walk beside me and be my friend.

—*Albert Camus*

*I*f you go looking for a friend, you're going to find they're very scarce. If you go out to be a friend, you'll find them everywhere.

—*Zig Ziglar*

*I*t is one of the blessings of old friends that you can afford to be stupid with them.

—Ralph Waldo Emerson

*I*f we would build on a sure foundation in friendship we must love friends for their sake rather than for our own.

—Charlotte Bronte

A friend is someone who gives you total freedom to be yourself.

—Jim Morrison

*E*very friendship travels at sometime through the black valley of despair. This tests every aspect of your affection. You lose the attraction and the magic. Your sense of each other darkens and your presence is sore. If you can come through this time, it can purify with your love, and falsity and need will fall away. It will bring you onto new ground where affection can grow again.

—*John O'Donohue*

A friend who is far away is sometimes much nearer than one who is at hand.

—*Les Brown*

To know someone here or there with whom you can feel there is understanding in spite of distances or thoughts expressed That can make life a garden.

—Johann Wolfgang von Goethe

I always felt that the great high privilege, relief and comfort of friendship was that one had to explain nothing.

—Katherine Mansfield

Friendship is a single soul dwelling in two bodies.

—Aristotle

*T*oo late we learn, a man must hold his friend Unjudged, accepted, trusted to the end.

—*John Boyle O'Reilly*

*T*wo persons cannot long be friends if they cannot forgive each other's little failings.

—*Jean de La Bruyère*

*O*ne measure of friendship consists not in the number of things friends can discuss, but in the number of things they need no longer mention.

—*Clifton Fadiman*

A friend is someone who knows all about you and still loves you.

—Elbert Hubbard

M y best friend is the man who in wishing me well wishes it for my sake.

—Aristotle

T he real test of friendship is can you literally do nothing with the other person? Can you enjoy those moments of life that are utterly simple?

—Eugene Kennedy

A true friend is one who overlooks your failures and tolerates your success.

—*Doug Larson*

F riendship is the inexpressible comfort of feeling safe with a person, having neither to weigh thoughts nor measure words.

—*George Eliot*

A friend is one that knows you as you are, understands where you have been, accepts what you have become, and still, gently allows you to grow.

—*William Shakespeare*

*F*riendship marks a life even more deeply than love. Love risks degenerating into obsession, friendship is never anything but sharing.

—Elie Wiesel

I don't believe that there is any true friendship without a bond of honor, and the honor in friendship is the respect you give the other that she also gives you.

—Dorothy Allison

Afterword

TRUE FRIENDS HELP US become the best version of ourselves—not the image we project at work or at family gatherings or on social media, but our authentic selves. They provide candor and insight; they encourage our talents and gently dust off the mirror so we can see our flaws. True friends accept us for who we are when we arrive on their doorstep, asking only for that same generosity of spirit in return.

This exchange seems simple enough, yet it's often difficult to find. How many people can you call up in the middle of the night when your car has broken down?

Whose voice can lower your blood pressure the second you hear it on the other end of the line?

We show our vulnerable side in our friendships. And when we're accepted, despite our quirks, we stand on firmer ground in all aspects of our lives. Through that we grow stronger, more confident and secure. Our true friends help us become the person we were meant to be—the person they've seen us as all along.